The Nature of Human Action

GRZEGORZ HOPPE

New York 2016

Copyright © 2016 Grzegorz Hoppe

All rights reserved.

New York 2016
ISBN:978-1537473147

For my wife Wiesia

CONTENTS

	Introduction	1
1	Ludwig von Mises's a priori axiom of human action	6
2	The hedonistic nature of human action	20
3	Study of consumer choices	51
4	The annoyance of work and social cooperation	58
5	The process of socialization as an exogenous factor limiting hedonism	62
6	The habit loop – a blessing and a curse	66
7	Limitations to the human pursuit of happiness	69
8	Hedonism in three dimensions	74
	Conclusion	77
	Bibliography	81

INTRODUCTION

> *There's no such thing as society.*
> *There are individual men and women and there are families.*
> Margaret Thatcher

Human decision making is one of the most important processes determining how the modern world economy manifests itself. What guides us in our everyday decisions to choose one product over another, what we regard as important (or not), what our priorities are and how these change over time are fundamental questions that we need answers to if we are to understand the many complexities of economic events. I will attempt to answer these questions with my own concept of the nature of human action and confirm the following hypotheses which arise from it:

T1: Human action is of a hedonistic nature, which implies a large number of theories in economics and management science and in particular allows many theories of consumer behavior to be confirmed.

T2: The hedonistic nature of human action is reflected in three spheres, personal, political and organizational, with political hedonism an inherent feature of the political classes, entailing negative consequences for the whole of society, in particular leading to the misallocation of all resources and the inability to achieve optimal quality of life.

In order to avoid semantic misunderstandings, a few introductory words are appropriate. Modern economics uses terms such as "social good", "social justice" or "social equality". One of the fundamental errors in many theories is to treat society as if it is an entity which actually exists.

> "Society" is sometimes treated as a superior or quasi-divine figure with overriding "rights" of its own; at other times as an existing evil which can be blamed for all the ills of the world. The individualist holds that only individuals exist, think, feel, choose, and act; and that "society" is not a living entity but simply a label for a set of interacting individuals. Treating society as a thing that chooses and acts, then, serves to obscure the real forces at work [Rothbard, 2004: 45].

In fact, there is no entity called society. What we are actually dealing with is a collection of individuals who belong, by virtue of an accepted criterion, to some social group. These are always, however, autonomous people with their own individual aims and who take their own, individual, usually completely different, decisions. Society is the same entity as the statistical resident or the statistical consumer who are not real beings but some form of conceptual generalizations, exploited for pre-defined research or statistical aims. The sociologist Arnold W. Green somewhat ironically sums up the issue:

> [S]ociety *is* whatever a total population *are* and *do*, no matter whether primary emphasis is placed upon persons or social relationships. It would follow, then, that if society is responsible for crime, and criminals

are not responsible for crime, only those members of society who do not commit crime can be held responsible for crime. Nonsense this obvious can be circumvented only by conjuring up society-as-devil, as evil being apart from people and what they do [Green, 1968: 656].

"Society" is therefore a collective notion, used to name a larger group of people. Synonyms for "society" are "family", "crowd", "gang" and other terms for a gathering of people. There are no grounds for personifying society since it is not a separate entity, and giving it the features of such would be an exaggeration. Society does not produce anything, nor does it discover anything or have the ability to procreate. There can be no concept of "society" in the sense of "metaphysical person" when we see that it disappears with the scattering of its constituent parts. As individuals disappear, so does the whole. The whole does not exist independently, and to use a collective noun with a verb in the singular leads us into an intellectual trap, since we have the tendency to personify the collective and ascribe to it its own body and mind [Chodorov, 1959: 29–30].

The above considerations clearly indicate that using the concept of "society" (as expressed by the noun "society" and the adjective "social") in economics is an exaggeration and serves only to deform reality. It is no great surprise that this concept is used by populist politicians. In the world of science, however, we should once and for all acknowledge that there are only individuals and they, through their independent and individual actions, make up the world economy.

These introductory remarks were intended to make clear that the economy can be considered exclusively the action of each person as an individual. The relevant aggregations of these actions may be made, but it must be borne in mind that that these are only the sum of the individual values, not values pertaining to social entities. Society does not make acts of choice, individuals do. Society does not aspire to happiness, individuals do and, what is more, happiness means something different to everyone. It is time to put an end to the popularization of metaphors so beloved of politicians (and also some economists), and demonstrate that the subjects of economic research are not unreal entities such as society, but individual human beings with their own problems, desires and activities which together make up social and economic reality. For this reason, further discussion will cover exclusively the actions of individual people, which is the foundation of praxeology, and therefore the science from which modern economics is derived[1]. Later, use of the term "society" will be in reference to a specific group of people, and will not denote a separate, independent entity.

In this book, the research methodology adopted is in accordance with that proposed by Imre Lakatos[2]. This system distinguishes a so-called metaphysical hard core from other theoretical propositions and auxiliary hypotheses which form a protective belt around the hard core. The assertions made in the hard core are an ontological constant, which undergoes affirmation and empirical confirmation of the hypotheses and propositions in the protective belt. The protective belt, made up of these auxiliary

---

[1] Such an approach is taken at least by the Austrian School
[2] **Imre Lakatos** (1922–1974) – a Hungarian philosopher of mathematics and science. His approach to the philosophy of science was an attempt to establish a consensus between Popper's falsificationism and the theory of scientific revolutions advocated by Kuhn. Lakatos sought a methodological approach which would allow the reconciliation of these conflicting positions. For Lakatos, what we consider "theories" are in fact groups of theories that refer to common ideas - the "hard core". These groups of theories Lakatos called "research programs" - scientists involved in a given research program should seek to protect the core from falsification by means of "auxiliary hypotheses".

hypotheses and theoretical propositions, assumes all possible tests and must be permanently adjusted or even changed so as to protect the hard core theses. A research program such as this is deemed successful if the whole procedure leads to a progressive problem shift, but fails if the problem shift is degenerative [Lakatos,1995: 73].

The research methodology adopted here results from a specific resource of contemporary knowledge and the interdisciplinary nature of research into the nature of human action. On the one hand, for over half a century we have had Mises's a priori axiom, which has not been challenged, and on the other an enormity of research on the principles of human action, carried out in various fields of science including economics, psychology, sociology, evolutionary biology and neuroscience. It is precisely this state of contemporary knowledge that tends towards treating Mises's axiom as a hard core theorem and surrounding it with auxiliary hypotheses (in the protective belt), using scientific achievements.

1. LUDWIG VON MISES'S A PRIORI AXIOM OF HUMAN ACTION

Human action, and above all acts of choice, are basic issues in the most universal science, praxeology. Within its framework, the area to have developed the most is economics. According to Mises, the correct approach to economic problems must begin with the study of acts of choice [Mises, 1998: 3]; for, if we want to construct any economic theories, we should always start from the principle that every person who is not in a vegetative state takes actions. Every moment of our life is an action, from birth to death. According to Mises,

> the starting point of all praxeological and economic reasoning, the category of human action, is proof against any criticisms and objections. No appeal to any historical or empirical considerations whatever can discover any fault in the proposition that men purposefully aim at certain chosen ends. No talk about irrationality, the unfathomable depths of the human soul, the spontaneity of the phenomena of life, automatisms, reflexes, and tropisms, can invalidate the statement that man makes use of his reason for the realization of wishes and desires [Mises, 1998: 67].

The fact that we use reason to achieve our goals is what, after all, sets humans apart from other organisms. Rationalism, praxeology and economics do not deal with the deeper motives of human action and its ultimate objectives, rather the means to be used to achieve a particular purpose. Regardless of the source of an impulsive need, the means for satisfying it are the result of rational thought on the effort required and the expected results [Mises, 1998: 16]. From an economic point of view, why we act is totally irrelevant. The sole point of interest is which means (resources) we use to reach our goals and whether the means used are optimal in the sense of their most favorable (lowest possible) expenditure.

Action is essential to the nature of our existence; it is a means to survive and rise above the level of the animal and plant kingdoms. Although an individual's achievements are impermanent and fleeting, for them, and for the studies they pursue, they are of paramount importance. Thanks to actions, humans set themselves goals and try to achieve them, and broaden their knowledge to explore the unknown. "Human action is necessarily always rational" [Mises, 1998: 18]. The ultimate goal, however, is to meet a need in the person acting. Due to the fact that one's own value judgments cannot be used in the assessment of actions taken by another, it makes no sense to pass judgment on the objectives and acts of the will of others. No one is capable of indicating what would make another person happier or less unhappy.

> The critic either tells us what he believes he would aim at if he were in the place of his fellow; or, in dictatorial arrogance blithely disposing of his fellow's will and aspirations, declares what condition of this other man would better suit himself, the critic [Mises, 1998: 16].

This is one of the most important principles, saying that

people are truly free, and can therefore make unrestricted acts of choice, and their choices can not be burdened with the prohibitions and dictates of others. This principle, which determines the level of subjective human happiness, is different for everyone. Nobody has the right to persuade another person that entering into possession of something or taking some specific action is good and will make them happy. Only a fool or someone who takes great pleasure in having power over others would think so.

In this context it is worth defining human action as the pursuit of happiness. This comes with a warning, however, against frequent misunderstandings. The ultimate goal of human action is always to satisfy the desires of the person acting. There is no criterion for greater or lesser satisfaction beyond an individual assessment of value, which varies from individual to individual, and also in the same person at different times of life. A person can say what causes them to feel more or less unpleasantness only on the basis of their desires and opinions as well as their own subjective judgment. No one has the right to decide what should make someone else happier. Otherwise, it must be accepted that most people are idiots who do not know what is good for them, with only an omniscient few with the right to determine what others should do and how they should live their lives. Economics and economists have no right to judge human action.

The problem now arises of introducing axiology to economics. Nothing and no-one entitles one person to judge what is good and what is bad. Each individual has a different scale of values, has different goals in life and different things make them happy. In economics, it is possible only to judge the means used to achieve the desired aims and indicate their rationality or optimality. Anyone who tries to define happiness is irresponsible, at the very least. There are as many concepts of happiness as there are people. True, many people have very similar or almost identical aims; this does not mean, however, that any generalizations may be made here. As previously indicated, just as in economics the concept of "society" should not be used, neither should one speak of what is good or bad for people in this respect. The only legitimate exception to this rule is valuation, but only for those goals which violate the principle of the integrity of another person's body or their property.

Economics does not assume that people aspire only or primarily to material prosperity, nor does it advocate them to do so. Economics as a branch of a more general theory of human action is involved in all human activity, which means the deliberate attempt by humans to set goals, regardless of what these are. It makes no sense to use the terms "rational" or "irrational" in relation to the goals people set themselves [Mises, 1998: 917]. Homo sapiens has never been, is not now, and never will be *homo economicus*. Of course there are bound to be some people among the seven billion on earth who match the definition since they are oriented towards maximizing possessions, but there is no reason to believe that everybody is like this. From all the human qualities, the most important is that everyone is different and that people differ in their goals, desires and needs and that they pursue these goals and desires in different ways. Some aim only to improve their living conditions; others are so preoccupied with their neighbors' problems that they treat them as if they were their own. For some, their greatest desire is to satisfy their sex drive, to eat well, have a drink, or own a beautiful house or other material goods. There are others, however, who are much more concerned with needs which are commonly known as "higher" or "spiritual". Some are quite happy to adapt to requirements, while others rebel against societal norms. Finally, there are also those for whom the ultimate goal of their journey on earth is eternal happiness, and those who profess no religion and are not guided in their actions by religious motives.

The idea that the incentive of human activity is always some uneasiness and its aim always to remove such uneasiness as far as possible, that is, to make the acting men feel happier, is the essence of the teachings of Eudaemonism and Hedonism. Epicurean *ataraxia* is that state of perfect happiness and contentment at which all human activity aims without ever wholly attaining it [Mises, 1998: 15].

It is precisely this unpleasantness which causes people to take action or refrain from it. If they did not feel any unpleasantness, it would mean that they are in a state of absolute happiness. This, however, never occurs, and unpleasantness probably disappears only with the cessation of life. So it can be assumed that as long as someone is alive, they perform a variety of actions. Of course, our actions do not always lead to the elimination of unpleasantness because our brains sometimes take inappropriate decisions which result in the unpleasantness remaining. This applies in particular to actions influenced by emotions, which specifically interfere with the cold logic of action. Action influenced by emotion is different from considered actions in terms of the evaluation of inputs and outputs: emotions interfere with the assessment of the situation, and to the person who is guided by emotions, and not by cool deliberation, the goals seem more desirable, and the efforts associated with achieving them smaller. Even in a state of emotional arousal means and ends are certainly taken into account, which shows that the costs of such behavior are higher [Mises, 1998: 16].

Emotions, however, are a natural part of the human condition, and also in this respect, nobody has the right to judge others. If someone uses inadequate resources to achieve their aims while in a state of emotional arousal, they do so at their own risk and bear the consequences of such an action. Everyone should have the right to free choice. We are free to preach our views on the dangers of tobacco[3], but we have to leave people the freedom to control their own lives.

> Otherwise, we may as well outlaw all sorts of possible carcinogenic agents – including tight shoes, improperly fitting false teeth, excessive exposure to the sun, as well as excessive intake of ice cream, eggs, and butter which might lead to heart disease. And, if such prohibitions *prove unenforceable*, again the logic is to place people in cages so that they will receive the proper amount of sun, the correct diet, properly fitting shoes, and so on. [Rothbard, 2006: 137].

It is freedom of choice that denotes human freedom. This kind of freedom does not exist in current social systems. Today, people are constrained by the countless dos and don'ts imposed by the ruling establishment on the rest of society although very often these rules do not apply to them. For among them are people who believe themselves to be "superhuman" and lay down the rules of life and conduct for the vast multitude of "simpletons". Does this mean, however, that people should have the unlimited right of choice? No, it does not, because no-one lives on a desert island where everything belongs to just one person and where it is not

---

[3] This applies to all intoxicants including alcohol, drugs etc.

necessary to worry about co-operating with others. However, there is nothing to prevent existing limitations arising only from the principle of the inviability of the body and property of others.

Today's world, though, is completely different. On the one hand, legal systems determine what we can and cannot do and are so highly sophisticated that it is possible to say that we are almost incapacitated. On the other hand, we have a ruling establishment, theoretically elected by us, which demands to be treated completely differently. Members of this group give themselves a raft of privileges which are unavailable to others, such as immunity protecting them from liability for breaching laws they themselves have created. Are they "super-humans"? Looking at their behavior, it is easy to come to the conclusion that they would like to treated as such.

The essence of human activity is described in detail in Ludwig von Mises's a priori axiom of human action. According to him, the axiom should become a basic paradigm of the economy, and also a starting point for describing a wide range of economic rights. The axiom is described by Hans H. Hoppe as follows:

> It is one of Mises's greatest achievements to have shown precisely that there are insights implied in this psychologically speaking trivial axiom of action that were not themselves psychologically self-evident as well; and that it is these insights which provide the foundation for the theorems of economics as true a priori synthetic propositions.
> It is certainly not psychologically evident that with every action an actor pursues a goal, and that whatever

the goal may be, the fact that it was pursued by an actor reveals that he must have placed a relatively higher value on it than on any other goal of action that he could have thought of at the start of his action. It is not evident that in order to achieve his most highly valued goal an actor must interfere or decide not to interfere (which is also an intentional interference) at an earlier point in time in order to produce a later result, nor is it obvious that such interferences invariably imply the employment of some scarce means – at least those of the actor's body, its standing room, and the time absorbed by the action. It is not self-evident that these means must also have value for an actor – a value derived from that of the goal – because the actor must regard their employment as necessary in order to effectively achieve the goal; and that actions can only be performed sequentially and always involve the choice of taking up that one course of action which at some given time promises the most highly valued results to the actor and excluding at the same time the pursual of other, less highly valued goals. It is not automatically clear that as a consequence of having to choose and give preference to one goal over another – of not being able to realize all goals simultaneously – each and every action implies the incurrence of costs (forsaking the value attached to the most highly ranking alter- native goal that cannot be realized or whose realization must be deferred) because the means necessary to attain it are bound up in the production of another, even more highly valued goal. Finally, it is not evident that at its starting point every goal of action must be considered worth more to the actor than its cost and capable of yielding a profit (a result whose value is ranked higher than that of the foregone opportunity), and that every action is also invariably threatened by the possibility of a loss if an actor finds in retrospect that contrary to his expectations the actually achieved result has a lower value than the relinquished alternative would have had. [Hoppe, 2011: 288–289].

Ludwig von Mises's a priori axiom of human action in the research methodology is a hard-core theorem. Put simply, the axiom can be determined by human subjectivity and the realization of human-designated goals while simultaneously mitigating any unpleasantness. This axiom can also be called the hedonistic principle of human action. Any theory that is inconsistent with it should be considered false. With the aim of better presenting this axiom, it is deconstructed and shown in graphical form below (Fig. 1.1.).

HUMAN ACTION AS THE PURSUIT OF SUBJECTIVE HAPPINESS

Each person aims for the goal to which, at the beginning of the action, they have subjectively ascribed the greatest value among all the goals they thought of at the beginning of the action.

To achieve this goal everyone needs to take action or refrain from acting, which means the use of scarce resources, e.g. at least the body of a given person and their time.

The resources used have a specific value for the person acting, and the person must be careful that the use of these resources is necessary to achieve the aim.

These actions must be performed one after the other in time and represent the choice of a course of action allowing for the achievement of the most valued goal and the exclusion from achievement of less desirable goals in the given time.

The result of prioritizing one goal over another is the incurrence of costs in the form of the inability to achieve alternative goals.

At the outset, each person must assign the selected goal a higher value than its cost and the expectations of the benefit (pleasure) from achieving the goal (goal evaluated through the value of achieving alternative goals).

Every action is threatened with loss if the person acting discovers in the future that the goal achieved has a value lower than that which would have been achieved by the alternative goal, which was abandoned.

Fig. 1.1. Graphical form of Ludwig von Mises's a priori axiom of human action.
Source: own work.

Humans act not only deliberately, since many of their behaviours are instinctive, or are emotional reactions and reflexes. These can be controlled and rationalized, however, and it is even possible to give up a strong instinctive need in order to be able to fulfill other desires. It follows that humans are not puppets in the hands of their desires: men do not throw themselves upon every woman they find attractive, nor do people devour every single last morsel of food if they feel a bit peckish or attack everyone they might feel like killing. They rank their wants and needs according to a certain scale and make decisions – in short, they act. And it is precisely this which differentiates humans from other animals; they can be aware of their behaviour and adjust it accordingly. They can restrain, control and even suppress their impulses and desires [Mises, 1998: 16]. This is how they regulate their desires and needs when they come into conflict with the protection of other people's property or their bodily integrity, refraining from action if this would be detrimental to the environment.

Freedom of choice and freedom to take action are subject to three types of restrictions. The first is the laws of physics: humans must adapt to their absolute inevitability if they want to live. The second is inherent individual qualities and characteristics, with environmental factors that influence both the choice of the means and the ends, although our knowledge of this subject is still inadequate[4]. The third is the regular relationships between the means and the end, i.e. the laws of praxeology, which differ from those of physics and biology [Mises, 1998: 793]. This regularity must not, however, be confused with a rule (theory). The fact that often- specified goals are related to specific actions provides no basis for the formulation of a general law. It is merely a kind of statistical regularity in the relationship between the means and the end with a specified likelihood in the past, which does not mean

---

[4] Filling the existing gap in this area is precisely the role of this article, and a closer examination of the issue will be undertaken in the next section.

that in the future it is not likely to change significantly. Reason and experience indicate the existence of two distinct spheres, an outer world of physical, chemical and physiological phenomena and an inner world of thoughts, feelings, judgments and purposeful action. With the current state of knowledge, it is impossible to identify a bridge linking these two spheres. It has been known for identical external events to cause differing reactions in people; at other times, two separate external events lead to the same reactions. It is not known why this happens, however [Mises,1998: 18].

This finding leads to the conclusion that the laws and theories of economics predict very little. Since it is impossible to induce identical reactions by way of specific external factors, it is also impossible to talk of a constancy of laws resulting from human action. Also, the fact that every person has their own definition of the happiness they are seeking means the same for prediction in economic theories, where the only constants appear to be variability and subjectivity.

Traditional economics does not occupy itself with either human behaviour or what people are like or how they act, but with a fictitious, hypothetical notion of them. Economics depicts humans as acting solely for economic reasons, that is, guided solely by the desire to obtain the greatest material or financial benefits. Critics of this approach claim that such people do not exist in the real world and that they are figments of the imagination of "armchair" philosophers. No-one is driven solely by the desire to make as much money as possible, and in fact many people have no interest in such petty considerations [Mises, 1998: 62].

The most significant fact in recent economic history, which may lead to the rejection of the concept of a rational *homo economicus,* was the award of the 2001 and 2002 Nobel Prizes for Economics to Joseph Stiglitz, Michael Spence, George Akerlof, Vernon Smith and Daniel Kahneman for, among other things, research on consumer behaviour in conditions of uncertainty and asymmetrical information. They proved that humans are neither rational nor objective, and that their decisions are guided by largely subjective considerations, including emotions.

All of the above does not negate the fact, however, that, despite their completely different goals, people still cooperate with each other. They do this out of self-interest, for it is only through cooperation and mutual assistance that can people achieve their aims easier and much faster than if they acted alone. Even if there was a natural innate hatred between various races, this would not prevent social cooperation [Mises, 1998: 171–173]. This cooperation, however, has nothing to do with love or the commandment that we should all love one another. People cooperate with each other in accordance with the principles of the division of labour not because they love each other or because they should do so; they cooperate because it is beneficial for them. Humans have complied with the requirements of social life, respect laws and the freedoms of others and have learned to replace hostility and and conflict with peaceful interaction. They have done so, however, not out of love or charity or even sympathy, but out of self-interest [Mises, 1998: 171–173].

A more accurate term in this case is, however, human hedonism, which is the engine of human action and the defining frame for each person's subjective definition of the happiness they aim for throughout their lives, although in all likelihood they never truly attain it, for once one goal is achieved, another one immediately takes its place. The human pursuit of the intangible state that is total happiness is never-ending. This continuous process of trying to pursue ever more needs (mitigating unpleasantness) is in fact an exciting quest to raise the standard (quality) of living. Fortunately, achieving a state of total happiness is impossible because this would entail a situation where a person has no new desires and feels no unpleasantness, which would resemble a state of oblivion, or death. It is impossible for the mind to comprehend, however, whether they constitute the highest form of happiness.

2. THE HEDONISTIC NATURE OF HUMAN ACTION

In my view, not only Ludwig von Mises's a priori axiom of human action but also my own concept of the hedonistic nature of human action, which is consistent with the axiom, may be helpful with regard to the economic considerations proposed in this work.

We should begin by recalling that as early as 1759, the father of modern economics, Adam Smith, in his Theory of Moral Sentiments, suggested that human economic behavior is based on two human psychophysical features:
- ➢ a tendency towards vanity, greed and laziness; and
- ➢ a tendency towards the division (specialization) of work.

Smith perceived humans as egoists, whose aim is to have the greatest amount of goods so as to be able to satisfy all their needs with as little effort as possible. According to Smith, people behave altruistically only when they can benefit from an action that does good to somebody else. His theories would still appear to have relevance today, apart from the assumption that all humans are egoists. It is my belief that human action is always hedonistic in character and, most importantly, that this is a positive phenomenon. With its focus on pleasure and benefits, human hedonism means that people set ambitious goals for themselves, and achieving them becomes the driving force in the development of civilization and frequently contributes to other people also obtaining pleasure or benefits.

The oldest form of hedonism to appear in the literature is Cyrenaic[5]. It can be described as a set of assertions:

- The only thing that counts is "private" happiness, i.e. individual egoism; other people's experiences are unknowable.
- Happiness can be achieved through momentary pleasures.
- What we call "long-term happiness" means a preponderance of pleasure over pain.
- Happiness is active i.e. an active state of mind/spirit/soul; however, this does not involve a lack of suffering.
- What are important are experiences in the here-and-now; what has been and what will be do not matter.
- Pleasure must be reconciled with reason, that is to say that it is not people who must submit to pleasure, but pleasure must submit to people. Pleasure is perfect when it can be experienced with no regrets or pain.

A modern definition of hedonism can be found in *The Time Paradox* by Philip Zimbardo and John Boyd. They consider that a hedonistic attitude is primarily characterized by people's focus on the present. Hedonists enjoy anything that brings them pleasure and avoid anything that might be a nuisance, they deliberately seek out pleasure and organize their lives around it. Above all, they focus on immediate gratification and short-term gains. They avoid situations that are tiresome and require effort, and also routine and boring activities [Zimbardo, Boyd, 2014: 106].

In contrast to the above definition, I see the hedonistic nature

---

[5] The Cyrenaics were a school of philosophy founded in the 4th century BC by Aristippus of Cyrene, a student of Socrates. Later, the doctrine became distorted and the school ceased to exist in the 3rd century BC. The characteristics of hedonism are taken from http://pl.wikipedia.org/wiki/Hedonizm (accessed 15.09.2014)

of human action as a mindset which aims at getting maximum pleasure or benefit regardless of the time when it occurs, and that each person defines their own pleasure or benefit in their own way, which translates into very different attitudes, among which are also altruistic attitudes, if this is the only way someone defines their benefit or pleasure.

Based on Mises's highly general axiom of human action and the definition of hedonism, I propose the adoption of the following detailed axiomatic hedonistic nature of human action:

> I. **Human beings try to achieve subjective and maximum subjective happiness or benefits by their actions.**
>
> II. **Humans have both a short-term and a long-term aversion to risk – this is a fear of the risk of not obtaining pleasure, or a benefit, or the fear of experiencing something unpleasant.**
>
> III. **When humans decide between immediate or long-term pleasures or benefits, they act so as to maximize gain.**
>
> IV. **Individuals arrive at their own subjective definition of pleasure and benefit, which may change during their lifetime due to the influence of their surroundings.**

V. **Every human action is determined by the functioning of both the unconscious and consciousness, with unconscious processes having priority when it comes to deciding on a given behavior.**

VI. **The human unconscious is always oriented toward achieving pleasure or a benefit, while consciousness is shaped over an individual's lifespan by their environment, i.e. by culture, religion, moral and legal principles, upbringing and learning, and this is why humans may display attitudes other than hedonism.**

VII. **The human unconscious is primarily shaped by drives and instincts (in particular by the sex drive, which causes the unconscious to seek sexual pleasure) [Hoppe, 2014: 17–24].**

These axioms may be called the primary determinants of human action in the choice of goals, and in the research methodology here adopted, there are supporting statements for a protective belt, which as such should be verified empirically. It should be stipulated that these result from economic theories and hypotheses which have already been empirically confirmed in numerous studies and are currently not questioned. They have become the basis for the formulation of specific axioms (auxiliary hypotheses). If we assume that these laws are correct, the complaint as to a lack of reasoning in the auxiliary hypotheses will be rejected. Included here are economic rights and hypotheses, in particular theories of consumer behavior, the most important of which are:

Hermann H. Gossen's law of diminishing utility

With the increasing consumption of a good comes a reduction in the increase of satisfaction with each subsequent unit of that good acquired. Consumers seek to split their income so that each monetary unit spent on the last unit of each good brings an equal increase in utility (satisfaction).

Ernst Engel's law

As income increases, expenditure on food as a proportion of total consumer expenditure is reduced.

John M. Keynes' absolute income hypothesis

As incomes rise so does consumption, but at a lower rate than the increase in incomes.

Milton Friedman's permanent income hypothesis

The level of consumer spending is not dependent on current disposable income but on long-term past average permanent income.

Veblen's paradox

In high-income social groups, higher prices for some goods cause demand for these goods to grow.

Franco Modigliani and Albert Ando's life-cycle hypothesis

The level and structure of consumer expenditure depend on the average income in the past, the current disposable income and expected future income for life.

James S. Duesenberry's relative income and irreversibility of consumption hypothesis

Satisfaction with consumption is largely dependent on the level of consumption in the surroundings, in particular on the social group which, consciously or unconsciously, is being followed. The level of one's own satisfaction with consumption depends on the consumption levels of the people being imitated. Where consumption levels are higher in the surroundings than in one's own group, the level of satisfaction with one's own consumption is reduced (the imitation effect). As incomes rise, consumer spending increases, whereas with a decline in income, consumers try to maintain their current level of consumption (the irreversibility of consumption, or the ratchet effect).

Tversky and Kahneman's prospect theory

The utility of objects does not depend on the general level of prosperity, but is relative. The initial level of satisfaction is irrelevant, and any deterioration is perceived as a loss, with the opposite, an improvement in the situation, perceived as a benefit. Entities are sensitive to changes in their situation, no matter their initial state, so even with an identical degree of intensity to the change, a deterioration is seen more acutely as a greater loss, and improvement in the situation as less benefit.

As a general rule, in economics we are dealing with the low predictive power of established laws[6], which is related to a lack in occurrence of identical external factors. This is somewhat different in the case of the theories above: they are well established, which means that they must be backed up by *something* with a constant (or almost constant) character. This constant *something*, I believe, is the hedonistic nature of human action, which has developed over the course of human evolution, always leading us to mitigate unpleasantness and aim for a state of subjectively-perceived happiness.

One may wonder whether the hedonistic nature of human action is a category of human nature, or a characteristic acquired in the process of obtaining self-awareness. In terms of the theory of human action, this question is gaining importance in the context of the difference between the descriptive and the normative approach in economics. If hedonism in human action is a category of human nature, we must take this into account in descriptive and normative economics[7]. Otherwise, we will be dealing with the hedonistic nature of human action in the descriptive approach, but in the normative approach this is not so clear. At this point, however, another question arises: according to the normative approach, can it ever be assumed that a person could be found who would not work in order to achieve a subjective pleasure or benefit and happiness at the same time? This seems highly unlikely, and therefore the two approaches would have to assume that human action has a hedonistic nature. Additionally, it should be noted that the human hedonism is endogenous and any possible limitations to it arise from exogenous factors occurring during the process of

---

[6] In the sense that they are used to predict the future

[7] Descriptive economics describes reality as it is, and normative economics evaluates facts and formulates judgments and analyses.

socialization.

This nature of human action arises from the study of evolutionary biology. This assumes that each individual organism is guided by self-interest, which stems from the principles of genetic evolution and the basic principle of the survival of the species. The concept of "self-interest" means nothing more than the intuitive desire of every organism to achieve the most optimal state, and therefore the intensification of pleasure and the avoidance of anything unpleasant [Schmidt-Salomon, 2013: 50]. The fact that we are guided by self-interest when making decisions also highlights one of the basic definition of economics, which is the act of buying and selling, usually understood by economists as a subjectively non-equivalent exchange. A clear example of this is when the two parties to a transaction are subjectively convinced they will obtain benefits for themselves.

It should also be noted that the hedonistic nature of human action can be both positive and negative for axiological purposes. As has already been stated, it is true that economics should be free of evaluation, but one can assume that each action can be negative, but only where the bodily integrity of another person or their property has been violated. Any other action must be regarded as positive, since it leads to the achievement of an individual's goals and thus to to their subjective sense of happiness.

This position can also be found in the history of philosophical thought. St. Thomas Aquinas defines good as what is desirable (*bonum est id quod est appetibile*). Friedrich Nietzsche disagreed with the view that good and evil can be in any way objectified, believing that these are always subjective and depend on the specific situation and environment. He argued that everything that we consider as a value is relative and subjective, and in particular moral values. There is no universally applicable objective morality; everyone has their own morality that suits their life goals and feelings [Nietzsche, 2009: loc. 113].

It should be also noted that with the development of ethical thought over the last two centuries there has been a dispute between utilitarianism and deontology. Utilitarianism implies that we should always strive for the greater good, meaning that we have to solve ethical dilemmas on the basis of an assessment of greater happiness (good), while deontologists express the view that some moral norms cannot be transgressed, and have rejected the argument that it is possible to achieve the greater good. These differing views have proved irreconcilable, so it is impossible to indicate a generally-accepted principle that says what is good and what is evil, what is moral and ethical, and what is immoral and unethical. Therefore, it is worth focussing on the issue of ethics and morality as separate concepts, since combining them leads to many misunderstandings and misleading statements on human action. Schmidt-Salomon highlights three major differences between the concepts:

> Firstly, morality is concerned with the *subjective evaluation of people* on the basis of criteria imposed allegedly by metaphysical instance ("Peter is good, Paul is bad!"), while ethics deals with an *objective assessment of the appropriateness of behavior*, while building on the intersubjectively-established rules of the game ("Peter took all the stakeholders' needs into account and acted honestly; Paul's behavior, meanwhile, was extremely unfair").
> On an ethical level, when we have conflicts of interest we try to look for solutions that equally satisfy all parties. To achieve this, we need not only to understand

the diverse needs of each party, but also know the exact causes of these conflicts. Furthermore, in complicated situations, we need to show a flexibility that will reconcile conflicting interests.

This kind of flexibility is not allowed by morality, because the principle of morality is not based on the rules of a game negotiated by individuals, but by religiously-shaped memeplexes[8] with an allegedly suprahistorical character. The moral notions of "good" and "bad" are such highly confusing metaphysical constructs that thanks to them, any group can almost arbitrarily discredit their opponents and put themselves in the best light.

[...] Secondly, reasoning from a moral perspective relates to the issue of personal responsibility in a given entity and is therefore inevitably based on the concept of free will, that is, on the assumption that under exactly the same conditions, this entity could have behaved differently than in it did in reality. Ethical (naturalistic) argumentation is not dependent on this type of problematic assumption, since it is principally only interested in the *objective responsibility* for potential or actual actions, and not the *subjective responsibility* (and therefore the free will) of the perpetrator.

---

[8] A memeplex is a shaped pattern of behavior resulting from the socialization process taking place over a long time period. It is the most common inter-generationally-transmitted pattern of conduct.

[...] Thirdly, the purpose of ethics is to seek fair solutions to conflicts of interest, and this makes sense only when the conflict concerns at least two parties with different points of view. One cannot behave unethically in relation to oneself. Moralists, however, argue on the basis of the memeplexes shaping them that "sinning" can also be against oneself, and that certain acts are immoral by definition – even if no-one is harmed (with the exception of the perpetrator). The difference between the moral and ethical position has far-reaching consequences for the human right to self-determination, which can be seen clearly in the realm of sexuality [Schmidt-Salomon, 2013: 162–163; author's translation].

Such a distinction between ethics and morality necessarily implies that science must reject the issue of morality and that the sole axiological criterion can only be ethics. In this situation, we must state emphatically that nobody has the right to claim the privilege to evaluate the actions of others by any moral measure. An important issue here would be an objective definition of good and evil, which is impossible. What for one person is good, might not be so for another. The same is true of evil, and it is precisely for this reason that I limit the evaluation of human action to the principles of the principles of the bodily integrity of another and of their property. Otherwise, this would mean, for example, solving a typical trolley problem[9], a thought experiment in which the

---

[9] The trolley problem is a thought experiment in ethics designed by Philippa Foot and later extensively analyzed by Judith Jarvis Thomson, Peter Unger and Frances Kamm. Along with philosophical considerations it also has applications

decision must be made as to whether to sacrifice the life of one person in order to save a greater number of people, or refrain from doing so in order to save one person but thus cause the deaths of several. Which solution is good and which is bad? They cannot be both good and bad, ethical and unethical.

Both human culture and the natural world are indeed full of cruelty, suffering and poverty, but these are not the result of the "terrifying power of evil", but the typical behavior of organisms caring for their own benefits and the effective operation of genetic and cultural replicators. "Good" and "evil" are meaningless notions that more confuse the picture of reality than assist in their understanding [Schmidt-Salomon, 2013: 85]. It is true that since its very beginnings, economics has been linked to ethics and philosophy, but the ethical approach postulated within it has always meant the adoption of an axiological, subjective perception of a phenomenon by a particular thinker. It is difficult to discern theories which would be regarded in the world of economics as objective and indisputable. In addition, it should be emphasized that we are not talking about the purpose of human action, but only its consequences. Every human, in their own way, decides the objectives of their action, but they all seek to obtain a subjective pleasure or benefit. So, from an economics point of view, the goals and motives of human action have no meaning, and the only thing that counts is the effects of this action. It is impossible for us to

---

in cognitive science and currently in neuroethics, analyzing philosophical issues from a neuroscientific view. It is also present in popular culture. It has triggered a whole class of theoretical problems used to analyze value systems, logical inconsistencies in thinking indicating unconscious moral axioms and to consider issues related to medicine, war and politics. What is the difference between killing someone and allowing them to die? Is it the effects which are always the most important, or the actions that we should never take regardless of the situation? The aim when analyzing such problems is the study of limits and the weaknesses of theories on issues related to ethics and morality.

know other people's motives, for every action hides other motives and objectives. All human beings are united only in the subjective pursuit of pleasure or benefits. In this sense, it does not matter whether and why there are people for whom, for example, an atavistic way of life is the goal of action. It must be accepted that this is simply the achievement of subjective pleasure. I believe, therefore, that describing the motives and objectives of all human action is beyond the capabilities of our knowledge, and creating various types of groupings for these phenomena has no cognitive sense, just as there is no sense in using the term "society". The hedonistic nature of human action has been *registered* in the human genome and may have led to the fact that humans, over the course of evolution, have become the dominant species on Earth[10].

In light of the above considerations, there are two types of hedonism in human action:

1. **Positive hedonism**, when the result of the action is something desirable and beneficial both for the person acting and their surroundings, or something desirable and beneficial only for that person and neutral for the surroundings,
2. **Negative hedonism**, when the result of the action is something desirable and beneficial for the person acting but is undesirable and unfavorable for the surroundings.

It should be noted that the more common type of hedonism in human action is positive[11].

---

[10] Contemporary humans are perceived in this way by evolutionary biologists.

[11] During a discussion on this issue, one of my friends asked me a trick question. "Do you think that Jesus was a hedonist, too?" I replied, "Yes, in the sense that he was trying to achieve a subjective pleasure or benefit. His aim,

The main assumption of the axioms introduced here is the acknowledgment of the universal subjectivity of all aspects of human perception, including the concepts of "pleasure or benefit" and "unpleasantness or loss". This also means that every individual has their own definition of happiness and goes down their own road in order to achieve it. Everyone is different and for this reason no-one may feel entitled to claim what is beneficial and what is detrimental to another.

These axioms require refinement and further description in order to avoid erroneous or ambiguous interpretations. Therefore, an interpretation of each of the axioms follows below, with examples to better illustrate each of these claims.

I. Human beings try to achieve subjective and maximum subjective happiness or benefits by their actions.

This means that each human being strives generally in all their actions to obtain a subjective pleasure or benefit. A subjective pleasure or benefit means a difference in perception and feeling of different sensations and material benefits by every individual. A pleasure may be both a physical and mental experience, for example, having sex, eating one's favorite food, listening to music, or helping someone else to win an award. A person subjectively

---

after all, was the salvation of mankind, and this could only be achieved with his death on the cross. So in this sense he was acting hedonistically, achieving his aim which was the salvation of mankind." We have to accept that hedonism is not *a priori* something negative; for very often something good and desirable comes out of hedonistic action. Hedonism as defined in this article may even mean the pursuit of one's own death in the name of the happiness of others, which is an example of extremely positive hedonism. Continuing with this argument, we can say that if humans were created in the image and likeness of God, the nature of human action must also have a hedonistic character. Of course, this last sentence is entering the metaphysical world and is not a scientific argument, only a loose conclusion in answer to the question.

perceives benefits in the same way: for one person, the most important benefit will be to get a luxury car, and for another a round-the-world trip, while for someone else it will be giving a gift. There will also be the person for whom a benefit will be to build a subjectively nicer home than the next-door neighbor's. For someone else, a benefit or pleasure may be not owning any goods at all. Max Scheler in 1912 observed that the average person, rather than experiencing values as such, evaluates them only "when comparing and by comparison" with the state of ownership, location, fate or qualities of other people [Scheler, 1998: 65], and therefore unpleasantness occurs only when referring to the situations of other people or other situations imagined as the ideal. This applies in particular when they are comparing their own situation to that of people in their immediate surroundings, and who are of similar social and material status. The issue of maximizing benefits is subjective and dependent on personal preference and the subjective evaluation of pleasure and benefits. Importantly, this axiom includes altruistic attitudes. It is not hard to find people for whom doing good gives the greatest pleasure. There are also those who, after achieving certain material benefits, revalue their preferences for pleasure and become altruists (on the outside). Is such behavior, however, the result of some kind of change in human nature? No, since it represents the fruits of evolution and adaptation to life in social groups. As Schmidt-Salomon states:

> The continuous increase in brain volume during hominid evolution was due to the fact "that the owners of more developed brains, thanks to their higher social intelligence, had an advantage over less-developed individuals. Understanding the multi-layered division of roles within social groups and the ability to use it in

their own interests meant a decisive advantage in the struggle for survival. Only those who could empathize with the needs of their companions knew when and with whom to cooperate, who could cheat with impunity, and who to flatter to get closer to their goal. These empathic abilities developed during the evolutionary process have become prerequisite skills for lying effectively, cheating, co-operating and hatching up intrigues and have created - as a side effect - a base for motivated compassion (and a common delight in) unselfish behavior. The unique human capacity for empathetically benefiting oneself is undoubtedly one of the nicest features of our species. We can not forget that this particular form of self-interest, motivating us again and again to perform unselfish acts, also has its limits. There is a significant difference between the suffering experienced personally and that to which we are only witnesses. The intensity of our sympathy, or our common enjoyment, is generally less than the suffering or the joy felt by those we are watching [Schmidt-Salomon, 2013: 55; author's translation].

The philosopher Ludwig Marcuse put the phenomenon as follows:

Sympathy is a more frequent occurrence than rejoicing. Why? Because it is easier for us to identify with other people's suffering than with their joy. Why? Because when we sympathize (suffer in common) we are also happy that taking a passive role is enough; meanwhile in rejoicing there is also a dose of suffering in that we are only complicit in it [Marcuse 1973: 84; author's translation].

Altruism, thus, is not, as we would wish, human action resulting from higher motives or a feeling of empathy for others, but simply action arising through evolution aiming towards the gaining of empathic benefit. Zygmunt Bauman believes that, as a rule, manifestations of human sacrifice, even if sincere, fervent and passionate, do not require personal sacrifice or dedication. People become involved in, for example, campaigns to protect the environment, but not involved enough to result in their leading a more modest life or even denying themselves the smallest pleasure. Not only do they not intend to renounce the pleasures of a consumer lifestyle, but often they do not even want to reconcile themselves to minor limitations of personal convenience. The driving force behind this seems to be the desire for fuller, more reliable and safer consumption [Bauman, 2009: 78].

II. Humans have both a short-term and a long-term aversion to risk – this is a fear of the risk of not obtaining pleasure, or a benefit, or the fear of experiencing something unpleasant.

This means that an important element of human action is to seek to minimize any kind of risk. Humans do not behave rationally, objectively optimizing their activities, nor do they choose the option of obtaining the greatest potential benefit if this is fraught with a risk that they are subjectively not prepared to take. A further important issue is the subjective perception of the probability of the event, which is not usually a mathematical probability. People have one approach to events of which the real (mathematical) chances of occurrence are medium or high, where they reduce the likelihood of their occurrence, and another where the likelihood is low, in which case they overestimate the chances they will happen. Also relevant is the time the event is expected to occur – negative events very distant in time are usually underestimated, and the real likelihood that they will occur is deemed irrelevant. This attitude means humans have a higher aversion to risk in relation to possible adverse events, including those with low probability, which will occur in the near future, and a lower aversion to risk in relation to negative events that may occur in the distant future. An example might be common unhealthy behaviors that bring people momentary subjective pleasure, e.g. alcohol, cigarettes, or casual relationships, and where any possible negative future consequences are underestimated, i.e. the subjective probability of their occurrence is low. On the other hand, when people buy lottery tickets, for example, in the days leading up to the draw they make plans for what they could do with the money – they overestimate the likelihood of a benefit. Even well-prepared students may underestimate their chances of exam success, and the chances of being fired from one day to the next may seem likely despite a lack of hard evidence. This may also apply to saving: in order to avoid unpleasantness due to a reduction in the future standard of living, which is an expression of aversion to the possible risk of future loss of income, people save part of their income for future consumption.

III. When humans decide between immediate or long-term pleasures or benefits, they act so as to maximize gain.

This means that human beings believe that they can rationally spread a pleasure or benefit over time so that it lasts as long as possible, and its total value is subjectively greatest. People can therefore give up all or part of a pleasure or benefit at the present time if they are convinced that giving it up now will bring a greater benefit in the future. An example of such behavior is the distribution of consumption over time, instead of spending all available income on achieving an immediate pleasure, which could ultimately lead to difficulties in the coming days in the form of an inability to meet basic physiological needs. People are also able to endure an inconvenience in the present or tolerate something unpleasant if it could contribute to obtaining greater pleasure in the future. This choice, however, is only possible when the total subjectively-expected value of pleasure will be higher than in the situation where there was no unpleasantness at the outset. An example of this may be the inability to purchase something desired at the present time, which brings a state of unpleasantness, but which is tolerated because of the chance to acquire something else in the future if the desire for this is even greater, and if having it will lead to greater satisfaction. Is this not why people choose not to purchase a large number of products they do not truly desire in order to save a larger amount of money to achieve their dreams?

IV. Individuals arrive at their own subjective definition of pleasure and benefit, which may change during their lifetime due to the influence of their surroundings.

This means that we are all different and that we perceive pleasure and benefit differently, which means that we desire different goods and different intangible assets. This is reflected in different tastes regarding material things (e.g. people buy different brands of cars) and intangible things (e.g. they listen to different types of music). This axiom also points to the influence of the surroundings on the changes that people undergo throughout their lives. What may be a pleasure or benefit early in life does not necessarily have to be so (and usually is not) at the end of it. Such changes also occur in terms of gaining social status, education, or with increasing wealth. Culture and religion also have a significant impact on an individual's definition of pleasure or benefit.

V. Every human action is determined by the functioning of both the unconscious and consciousness, with unconscious processes having priority when it comes to deciding on a given behavior.

This means that human actions are conditioned by processes occurring both in the unconscious and in the consciousness. The unconscious processes are primeval, and are based primarily on instincts, impulses, emotions and cognitive maps, which are a reflection of shaped habits. The processes of the unconscious are beyond our sensory perception, but they are responsible for most of our final decisions and choices. Unconscious ideas, including wishes, have no relation to reality. They are constantly active, regardless of the current external situation and the realistic possibilities that they can be achieved, and their relevance with e.g. the moral standards or the interests of the individual. It is estimated that less than 0.1 % of all brain activity reaches consciousness, and therefore more than 99.9 % escapes our attention. This is actually a good thing because humans have a relatively small working memory, and our awareness would be overloaded by the influx of large amounts of data which the brain processes every second [Kast, 2007: 75].

VI. The human unconscious is always oriented toward achieving pleasure or a benefit, while consciousness is shaped over an individual's lifespan by their environment, i.e. by

culture, religion, moral and legal principles, upbringing and learning, and this is why humans may display attitudes other than hedonism.

This means that our unconscious is always, and immediately, focused on the achievement of the pleasure or benefit. The unconscious always pushes us to act purely hedonistically. Awareness, under the influence of the unconscious, is shaped over our entire lifespan, and is subject to change during the socialization process. The most important factors shaping it include the culture, religion and moral customs prevailing in any given society. The impact of the surroundings on human consciousness means that some decision-making processes or decisions made at the level of consciousness will have a character other than purely hedonistic, or at least not give the impression they will be hedonistic. This results in an informed choice of action that brings unpleasantness (or at least a lack of pleasure), and which an individual accepts only due to the strong influence of the environment. Such behavior usually stems from established cultural patterns, which "force" us into taking unprofitable action. We act in this manner since we are guided by the principle of avoiding the unpleasantness which we could experience if we acted in opposition to the established cultural principles.

VII. The human unconscious is primarily shaped by drives and instincts (in particular by the sex drive, which causes the unconscious to seek sexual pleasure).

This means that, unconsciously, we aim primarily to achieve impulses and instincts. Particularly strong is sexual desire, which results in people trying to achieve sexual satisfaction despite the generally-accepted moral norms or ethical principles in their society. This urge is so strong that a person can be subject to it despite the negative consequences associated with it, and can therefore lead unintentionally to unpleasantness, both immediately after the desire is satisfied, and in the future, e.g. by contracting a sexually transmitted disease, or where a child is conceived to two people who are also in other relationships. If people did not have instincts and drives, there would be a high probability that the highly-developed society in which they lived would already be doomed to extinction, since conscious acts of procreation in such a society could be very rare indeed.

This axiom is thus based primarily on the results of the research and theories of Sigmund Freud. His best-known concept assumes that human action is the result of internal motivational forces which often come into conflict with each other and which are generally unconscious. These motivational forces are primarily instincts and needs. Since people are unaware of them, they often have no idea why they behave in one way rather than in another.

This view, as we know, became the foundation of psychodynamics. Freud's legacy remains to this day in concepts on the role of unconscious motivation, and the idea of defense mechanisms. He also proved that the first years of life have a decisive influence on the formation of human personality [in Kozielecki, 2000: 98]. Psychoanalysts, the supporters of psychodynamics, distinguish two types of instincts, primary and secondary. Primary, otherwise known as congenital, instincts are:

> ➢ efforts to obtain food,
> ➢ a desire to maintain an optimum body temperature,
> ➢ the sexual drive,
> ➢ avoidance of pain,
> ➢ a need for stimuli and contact with the outside world

[in Kozielecki, 2000: 101].

Secondary impulses arise during the socialization process. There is a very large number of them, including the need for security, interpersonal contacts or personal needs. The latter include, for example, the need for prestige, recognition and power.

In Freud's concept of instincts, a highly important role is played by defense mechanisms. To some extent these protect a person's "self" from fear, guilt, hopelessness or emotional disorders. The most important of these mechanisms are repression, rationalization, projection and substitution. Defense mechanisms act like habits, allowing humans to cope with a conflict situation, are unconscious and develop during the socialization process. Repression involves removing thoughts of failure and conflict from the consciousness, along with instincts and feelings that evoke fear or guilt; repression should be distinguished from suppression, which is a conscious reaction. Projection is another Freudian mechanism whereby a person ascribes their own undesirable attributes to others in order to reduce the fear of admitting that they are acting in a socially unacceptable manner, in accordance with the rule that "if others are like this too, then I am not doing anything wrong". Here people unconsciously assign to other people characteristics that they do not actually have. Another defense mechanism is rationalization, in which people supply untrue or incomplete motives to their actions. This is a kind of "moral cleansing" of the motives behind one's behavior for the benefit of others in the surrounding environment. People usually declare that they are doing something for others, or for the common good, while their real motivation is purely hedonistic. The last of the mechanisms is substitution, which takes two forms, compensation and sublimation. Compensation involves directing one's activity toward achieving goals that are similar to those could not be achieved or which cause anxiety. This mechanism can lead to very positive changes; for example, a student may turn his or her failure in sports into success in science. Meanwhile, sublimation is the transformation of one's failures into creative imagination and the world of fantasy. It can also lead to socially positive changes; for example, this is how one's creative abilities can develop.

The overview of defense mechanisms shows that their formation is very often caused by hedonistic behaviors that are negatively perceived by society. Those who do not want to admit to themselves or to the people in their surroundings that they are behaving in a hedonistic way create the mechanism of repression or rationalization. Psychoanalysts point to the current issue of consumerism. They believe that this phenomenon is also a kind of defense mechanism against anxiety. Consumption is a means of avoiding unpleasantness and protecting oneself from, for example, loneliness or a lack of love, or of fulfilling the need to increase one's prestige or self-esteem [Hoppe, 2014: 64–65]. We must also not forget about the human realm of feelings and emotions. If a person feels no emotion, they are unable to make choices. In the neuroscientist's view it is understandable that in decision-making processes emotions play a major role – the emotional advantage over rationality is determined by brain physiology. It is worth quoting here Gerhard Roth, in whose opinion:

> [...] it is the limbic system, not the cerebral cortex, which has direct access to these systems in the brain that ultimately affect our behavior. [...] In disputes with the rational cortex the first and last word belong to the limbic system. The first, from the moment when our desires and intentions are born; the last when deciding as to whether and in what form whatever sensible reason came up with is to be achieved. This is due to the fact that everything common sense suggests must be emotionally acceptable for the individual making

the choice. There are rational discussions about alternative behavior and the resulting consequences, but there is no such thing as rational behavior. Even the longest decision-making process always ends with an emotional for and against [Roth 2003: 162].

All of the foregoing axioms relate to principles of evaluating needs in accordance with Abraham Maslow's hierarchy of needs. This theory states that human needs are organizes hierarchically, and that subsequent needs can be met only when a need on a lower level has been met. Maslow's hierarchy of needs is shown in Figure 2.1. As can be seen, lower order needs arising from human instincts and drives are first to be met. One of the most important is the instinct to preserve life, which determines much of human behavior. This important principle must be specifically taken into account when analyzing the actions of those who suffer from a shortage of basic goods, because their activities will be significantly different from the activities of people living in prosperity.

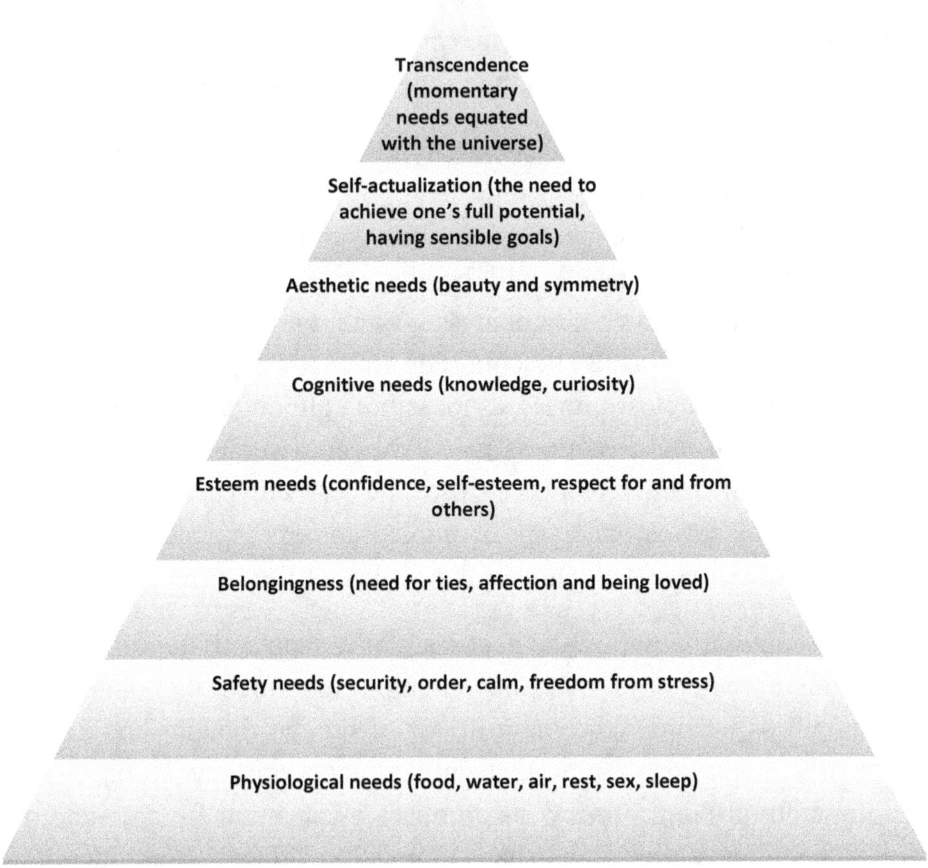

```
                    Transcendence
                    (momentary
                    needs equated
                    with the universe)

              Self-actualization (the need to
              achieve one's full potential,
                having sensible goals)

          Aesthetic needs (beauty and symmetry)


           Cognitive needs (knowledge, curiosity)


      Esteem needs (confidence, self-esteem, respect for and from
                            others)


      Belongingness (need for ties, affection and being loved)


       Safety needs (security, order, calm, freedom from stress)


        Physiological needs (food, water, air, rest, sex, sleep)
```

Fig. 2.1. Abraham Maslow's hierarchy of needs.
Source: Own work based on Maslow, 1970.

Furthermore, while all the desires and needs of people may be physical and psychological, lower-level needs are usually physical, whereas higher-level needs are usually psychological. This translates to the fact that unpleasantness may take both physical and psychological forms. In the case of psychological unpleasantness, these stem from a lack of achievement of specific needs and desires, and from comparisons with the state of ownership, location, fate or qualities of others. This kind of unpleasantness is a common and widespread phenomenon and has consequences in the form of striving for equality with other people, especially those who are in the immediate surroundings.

Referring Maslow's hierarchy of needs to Mises's axiom, we can say that it also represents a kind of hierarchy of unpleasantness. The person who feels unpleasantness associated with their lowest needs will be the most disadvantaged. If we assume that the level of happiness is equal to the level of quality of life, and define this as the condition in which a person is affected by as little unpleasantness as possible (although it is important what kind of unpleasantness it is), we can assume that the higher the level of quality of human life, the less unpleasantness is felt (where the lowest category of unpleasantness is important). The higher the category, the higher the quality of life.

Similar views on the hedonism of human activity are held by Bauman, who says that the situation in which the pursuit of happiness becomes the main driver of human thought and action heralds a veritable cultural, social and economic revolution. From the cultural point of view, it promises a transition from a state of unchanging routine to constant innovation, from the reproduction and maintenance of "what was" in a state "which was" to create and / or seize "what no one has ever seen or had before." From being pushed to being pulled, from needs to desires. From causal motivation to motivation by a goal. From a sociological point of view it coincides with a movement leading from governments of tradition to "the dissipation of everything permanent into the air and the profanation of everything holy." From an economic point of view, it will lead to a retreat from meeting needs towards the production of desires [Bauman, 2009: 57-58]. The author adds that uncertainty is a natural feature of human life, and the hope of getting rid of uncertainty the primary driving force of human action. Getting rid of this condition is an essential, even if only tacitly assumed, component of any vision of happiness. This is why "real, perfect and complete" happiness is always just in front of us, like the horizon, which, as we know, moves away when we try to get close to it [Bauman, 2009: 41]. Alexis de Tocqueville, writing about the psychological impact of the "pursuit of happiness", which has been raised to the rank of a right, obligation and the overarching goal of human life, recognizes the problem in this way:

> It perpetually retires from before [Americans], yet without hiding itself from their sight, and in retiring draws them on. At every moment they think they are about to grasp it; it escapes at every moment from their hold. They are near enough to see its charms, but too far off to enjoy them; and before they have fully tasted its delights they die. To these causes must be attributed that strange melancholy which oftentimes will haunt the inhabitants of democratic countries in the midst of their abundance, and that disgust at life which sometimes seizes upon them in the midst of calm and easy circumstances [Tocqueville 2008: loc. 2146].

Similarly Bauman comments on the freedom of human action in the name of their own well-being which, according to him, is a natural way to prosperity in the general public. He argues that:

> [...] the escape route from the nightmare of war, cruelty and violence leads through rebirth and liberation in human selfishness, that natural feature which certainly refers to every individual, if only such a possibility arises. Let people succumb to the natural tendency to take care primarily of their own well-being, comfort and pleasure, which give a sense of happiness, and after some time they will discover with certainty that murder, rape, theft and cruelty do not serve their interests. From the Kantian perspective of "categorical imperative" Reason will tell them that their self-interest requires them to do to others only what we wish to experience from others, and refrain from doing what they do not want to experience, that is, to respect the interests of other people and do not give in to the temptation to harass them and covet their property [Bauman, 2009: 92, author's translation].

To sum up the considerations in this section, it should be added that my own axiom of human action is largely consistent with Ludwig von Mises's a priori axiom, from which it is derived. These links are reflected in the methodology adopted here: the axiom of human action is the protective belt for the "hard core" theorem, i.e. Mises's axiom. My own auxiliary hypotheses in the protective belt are to be that part of the accepted theory of human action which is to resist all attacks on the hard core theorem.

The analysis of Mises's axiom leads to the conclusion that human action to eliminate unpleasantness is synonymous with action to achieve pleasure or benefit, since the mitigation of unpleasantness always leads to a state of greater pleasure. Every time a person gets rid of some unpleasantness, they get closer to subjectively-determined happiness. Do people always act optimally and get closer to happiness? Of course not – the feeling of free choice, however, is a hundred times more important for them than the awareness of making the best choice that would not be their choice. They would, then, always experience unpleasantness in the lack of freedom, thinking that free choice would be more beneficial for them[12]. For free choice in all aspects of human life is an important component in feeling full freedom, as well as the source of the formation of pleasure or benefit. Hence any limitation is understood as a loss of joy or happiness and a reduction in the quality of life. In this way, everything that restricts people's free choice becomes incompatible with their desire for happiness, the nature of their existence and the nature of their every action. All such restrictions must be, and are, seen as actions against a maximum level of happiness, and measures restricting free choice should be identified as incompatible with the nature of human action and as obstacles to happiness. Although individuals have differing concepts of happiness and the way to achieve it, any limitations on free choice always conflict with this desire and hamper the process. At the same time, we must note that in order to have free choice in our actions, the following conditions must be fulfilled:

1. We must be aware of what options for behaviour in a given situation are available; the greater the number of options, the higher the probability that we will take a sensible, independent decision. When there is just one option, the freedom to decide is small.

---

[12] It is less unpleasant for us to lose $100 in the casino than have $100 stolen from us.

2. We must be able to assess the possible consequences of using each option to determine which of them will be most beneficial for us. Each solution involves another type of costs and brings various benefits, both for ourselves and for others. In order to rationally assess both, the brain does not only need the necessary information to do so, but also must be able to process them to the benefit of the intended purpose.
3. We must have the means to actually allow us to pursue our preferred option [Schmidt-Salomon 2013: 135].

If a person finds themselves in a situation when the above conditions are met, their freedom of choice may be affected by internal factors (socialization processes) and external factors, i.e. the system of law created by the state.

3. STUDY OF CONSUMER CHOICES

The multiplicity of laws and hypotheses in economics on which I have based my axiomatic concept of human action (one of the subjects of this article), certainly may indicate in its favor and confirm its legitimacy. For additional verification of the concept, an experiment was conducted on consumer choices in 2010-2012 [Hoppe 2014: 72-76]. This was not intended to confirm all the axioms (auxiliary hypotheses), but only the following:

- ➢ Human beings try to achieve subjective and maximum subjective happiness or benefits by their actions.
- ➢ Humans have both a short-term and a long-term aversion to risk – this is a fear of the risk of not obtaining pleasure, or a benefit, or the fear of experiencing something unpleasant.
- ➢ Individuals arrive at their own subjective definition of pleasure and a benefit, which may change during their lifetime due to the influence of their surroundings.
- ➢ The human unconscious is always oriented toward achieving pleasure or a benefit, while consciousness is shaped over an individual's lifespan by their environment, i.e. by culture, religion, moral and legal principles, upbringing and learning, and this is why humans may display attitudes other than hedonism.

The research method
The experiment was based on a comparison of consumer choices

made during a pre-holiday period (Christmas) by a group of participants (approx. 150 people) with similar incomes and with the same amount of money at their disposal, PLN 300-350. The homogeneity of the group in terms of income was important for evaluating potential consumer choices, which, theoretically, would be close to each other. With a wide distribution of incomes it can be expected *a priori* that there will be differing purchasing preferences.

Importantly, the participants were not aware that their consumer choices were under scrutiny, which ensured that they maintained natural consumer behaviour. The purchases had to be made in one particular hypermarket within a four-week period. All of the participants were required to spend the entire sum (in the form of gift vouchers) in one shopping trip, with any unused portion of the vouchers forfeited. After all the participants had been on their shopping trip, a summary was compiled of the purchases made, on the basis of which their consumer choices were analyzed in order to confirm or reject the hypotheses.

In the interests of research objectivity, I should like to point out a problem which was the lack of precise knowledge as to the economic and social situation of all the participants' households, where some purchasing decisions may have been made precisely due to these situations. On the other hand, what was known was the income situation of those participants directly involved in the study, which I also consider important. Other strengths of this experiment were the participants' lack of awareness as to its procedure and the factual, and not declarative, choice of products through their actual purchase. These circumstances serve the aim of the study, which was to reflect the participants' actual acts of choice.

The experiment

1. The sample group consisted of approx. 150 employees at one company who were at a similar income level, earning around the national average monthly salary, i.e. approx. PLN 3,600 gross.
2. Each member of the sample group received vouchers to an identical value (PLN 300–350) to be exchanged in the 3–4 weeks before Christmas in one hypermarket for any goods available in the store.
3. The study was repeated three times over the years 2010, 2011 and 2012.
4. The material for the analysis was the receipts from all the members of the research group for all their purchases and summary statements from the hypermarket.
5. The participants did not know that their shopping decisions were the subject of the study.

The research hypotheses

In accordance with the accepted axiom of human action, the following research hypotheses were proposed:

H1: All the receipts will differ as to the products purchased, i.e. there will be no two identical receipts with the same products listed.

Confirmation of this hypothesis would mean that every human being has different, subjective preferences and different, subjective priorities in terms of the products they purchase. This may also be considered as evidence for the irrationality of consumer choices and a lack of desire to achieve the objective maximization of utility.

H2: To a large extent, the products purchased will have no utilitarian function related to meeting physiological needs, but will be "pleasurable" products. This will apply both to food and non-food items. There will be low repeatability in the products.

Confirmation of this hypothesis would indicate that people seek to obtain pleasure. Low repeatability in the products may be an additional argument for subjectivity in definitions of pleasure.

H3: The value of the unused vouchers will be low, at less than 1 %.

Confirmation of this hypothesis would mean that the axiom on the human aversion to the risk of unpleasantness would be confirmed. Here, the unpleasantness would be losing a significant part of the voucher value through making inappropriate product choices.

Results

The basic values and indicators obtained from the analysis of the source material used in the study are shown in Table 3.1.

Table 3.1. Summary of results

Year	2010	2011	2012
Number of participants in the research study	148	143	140
Value of the vouchers per one participant in PLN (USD)	350.00 (approx. 114.00)	350.00 (approx. 114.00)	300.00 (approx. 98.00)

Total value of the vouchers in PLN (USD)	51,800.00 (approx. 16,873.00)	50,050.00 (approx. 16,303.00)	42,000.00 (approx. 13,681.00)
Total value of the purchased products in PLN (USD)	51,541.62 (approx. 16,792.00)	49,834.87 (approx. 16,233.00)	41,733.91 (approx. 13,594.00)
% of unused funds	-0.4988%	-0.4298%	-0.6335%
Total number of different products purchased (pieces)	4,801	3,993	3,528
Total number of products purchased, in pieces (sold by the piece)	8,553	7,042	6,241
Total weight of products purchased in kilograms (sold by weight)	840.17	676.53	474.50
Average number of different products purchased by one participant	32.44	27.92	25.20
Average total number of products per participant (1 pc. = 1 kg)	63.47	53.98	47.97
Total number of products bought as single pieces (% of the number of all different products)	2,749 (57.26%)	2,247 (56.27%)	2,060 (58.39%)
Percentage (%) of products purchased at the standard VAT rate	50.82%	52.00%	51.57%
Percentage (%) of products at a reduced VAT rate	49.18%	48.00%	48.43%
Average value of one product in PLN and USD	5.49 (approx. 1.79)	6.46 (approx. 2.10)	6.21 (approx. 2.02)
Number of different products of which at least ten pieces were purchased (% of the number of all different products)	69 (1.44%)	54 (1.35%)	58 (1.64%)
Number of different products of which at least ten kilograms were purchased (% of the number of all different products purchased)	11 (0.23%)	6 (0.15%)	4 (0.11%)

The average number of different products offered by the store used in the study was between 55,000 and 60,000. All the products were sold in two units of measurement only, i.e. pieces and kilograms.

For the purpose of analyzing the source data the following assumptions were made in order to make the statistical calculations:

- In order to convert the units of measurement, it was assumed that 1 piece = 1 kilogram, but calculations concerning single items were only made for items whose quantity was expressed in pieces.
- Products purchased in larger quantities were those of which ten or more pieces, or ten or more kilograms, were purchased.

The conclusions arising from the analysis of the data in the table above and the source data are as follows:

1. In any year of the study no two identical sets of products were purchased by different participants, which means that hypothesis H1 can be confirmed.
2. The value of the vouchers forfeited due to an inaccurate selection of products in terms of their total value ranged from 0.4 % to 0.6 % of the overall value of the vouchers, which means that hypothesis H3 can been confirmed.
3. Statistically, each of the participants purchased from 25 to 32 products which were not purchased by any of the other

participants, which means that there was a variety of purchasing preferences and a high variety in terms of subjective definitions of benefit. This serves as confirmation of hypotheses H1 and H2, and is also consistent with the definition of the act of sale as a subjectively nonequivalent exchange.

4. Statistically, in all the years, over 50 % of each shopping cart contained products which were not repeated in any other shopping cart, which is also confirmation of hypotheses H1 and H2.
5. Given that the products taxed at the standard rate accounted for more than half of all purchases, and that this rate applies to highly-processed products (food), and the majority of non-food products, this means that most of the goods purchased did not serve to meet basic needs and were "pleasurable", which confirms hypothesis H2.
6. Products of which 10 or more pieces or 10 or more kilograms were purchased accounted for less than 2 % of all products, which is a sign that repeatability in the products was low and confirms hypothesis H2.

The results obtained from this study are thus consistent with the hypotheses, meaning that they can be confirmed.

4. THE ANNOYANCE OF WORK AND SOCIAL COOPERATION

The basic thesis of praxeology states that people prefer whatever gives them more satisfaction over what gives them less satisfaction, and that are inclined to assess the value of given things on the basis of their usefulness. This thesis contains a theorem, therefore, that human beings prefer work only in the situation where its benefits are more desirable than the enjoyment of leisure [Mises, 1998: 131-132]. This is a highly important trait of human nature, which manifests itself in many aspects of human life and the nature of human decision making. To put it colloquially, humans are by nature lazy and will always, wherever possible, give in to pleasure and avoid work.

This praxeological statement is consistent with the axiom of human action discussed in this work. People seek subjective benefits or pleasure, and avoid loss or unpleasantness. Only when the benefits of work translate into pleasure, the work itself compensating unpleasantness, will they be willing to undertake it. This feature is also of great importance for the development of civilization. People wanting to limit the unpleasantness of work compete to continuously improve the production processes all goods, seeking the smallest role for human labor and creating increasingly efficient manufacturing processes. It can thus be assumed that the hedonistic nature of human action and the resulting feeling of unpleasantness of work are the driving force in the development of civilization.

Work is regarded as something unpleasant and the state of not having to work is considered more satisfying. With no change in any other conditions, people prefer leisure than work. They work, however, when they value the income gained through work over the fall in contentment caused by the reduction in leisure. From this perspective, working is seen as an annoyance [Mises 2011: 131-132].

Just such a state has led to a situation whereby, in highly developed economies, the past few centuries have seen a steep decline in work time. This fact has a double meaning for both people and economic development. On the one hand, we can relax more, and on the other a gap in the market has been created which has gradually been filled by a range of new leisure-based services for those who are willing and able to indulge in ever more numerous pleasures. This can be seen in particular with the development of the tourism, leisure and health and wellbeing sectors, which includes spas.

Of course, there are people for whom work is not unpleasant; however, these people are few and far between. From the many millions of people in existence, there are individuals whose achievements and ideas carve out new paths for humanity. For such geniuses, creating is the essence of life. What exactly they do, however, is not quite the praxeological concept of work. It is not work, because from a pioneering genius's point of view, work is not a means to end, but an end in itself [Mises, 2011: 139]. We are, therefore, referring to those who create a new reality and, in fact, new possibilities for the development of civilization, leading to an even greater reduction in the amount of work for the remaining people. This fact is not relevant to the accepted axiom because, for these outstanding people, work is simply a pleasure, which in this sense seems to be consistent with the nature of human action.

Another issue related to the annoyance of work is working with others. Long ago, humans came to the conclusion that they are not self-sufficient and that by working together they can achieve much more. Thus was born the division of labor, which does not result from a need to cooperate with others but from pure hedonism, as it requires people to work together to improve their own existence. Each step towards the replacement of individual human activity by interaction with others results in an immediate, visible improvement in the situation. The benefits of peaceful cooperation and division of labor are widespread, and have an immediate impact on every current generation, not just subsequent generations. Sacrifices demanded of individuals for the good of society are rewarded with interest; however, this sacrifice is illusory and short-term, since the long-term future gain is greater than the loss caused by the sacrifice. This is quite obvious to every reasonable person [Mises 1998: 146]. Therefore, in fighting for their own best interests, individuals are working for the development of social cooperation and peaceful coexistence. Society is a product of human action, the result of people's efforts to remove unpleasantness from their lives [Mises, 1998: 146].

The division of labor has led to an incredible increase in productivity and efficiency, which has resulted in the current standard and quality of life. If (and to the extent to which) work under the system of the division of labor is more productive than isolated work and if (and to the extent to which) a person is capable of noticing this fact, they will aim to act cooperatively and associate with others.

Today we speak not so much of the division of labor as of knowledge. The development of all fields of science has led to the situation that the average person has no chance of having complete, up-to-date knowledge in many areas. People are in some ways condemned to each other, since they have to use the knowledge of others in order for science to develop further. Friedrich Hayek stated that civilization begins when people, in the pursuit of their goals, can use more knowledge than they possess, and when they cross the boundaries of their ignorance through the use of knowledge which they do not have [Hayek, 2005: 42]. Humans become social beings not because they sacrifice their own needs in the name of a mythical deity called society but because they have the desire to improve their own lot in life [Mises 1998: 160]. The formation of social systems is the natural evolution of human life. In the name of self-interest, people seek to cooperate and have good relations with others.

5. THE PROCES OF SOCIALIZATION AS AN EXOGENOUS FACTOR LIMITING HEDONISM

As stated in my 6th axiom, the human unconscious is always focused on the achievement of a pleasure or benefit, while consciousness, shaped as it is by the process of socialization over a lifetime, by culture, religion, moral and legal principles, upbringing and education, may result in attitudes other than hedonistic. Are people's actions always driven by the principle of benefit? Of course not – they act that way only at the start of life, as later they are subject to the influences of the socialization process which leads to changes in actions.

The most important factors influencing changes in human action are the religion, culture, moral norms and legal system in force or accepted in any given society. Life within social structures has led to much unnatural behavior in individuals, for moral, cultural and legal principles very often contradict the hedonistic nature of human action. The result of this situation is that many people live in a state of permanent hypocrisy, and not just in relation to others. People have great difficulty being assertive and very often what they say is not what they think, and in many situations they behave completely differently than how they had intended. The axiomatic nature of human action is affected. Added to this, in many cases they cease to act in accordance with the principle of benefit, and stop seeking pleasure or benefit. Sometimes, even consciously, their action brings them unpleasantness because, as a result of socialization processes, the power of the environment is so strong that they cannot fight it. They are then faced with dilemmas such as, "It's just not done," "It wouldn't be right," or "What will others think?" They cease to be themselves, and stop pursuing their own way to happiness.

This does not mean, however, that the process of socialization has only a negative impact on human action. If that were so, people would not be able to live in social structures, which is a necessary condition for the pursuit of happiness. In many cases, they must consciously give up the immediate benefit or pleasure to be able to get more of it at a later date. It must not be forgotten that social cooperation led to the development of civilization and to the division of labor, with the result that we now have a much higher standard of living than in the past. In relation to the negative impact of socialization, I have in mind factors including:

- the impact of existing legal rules that restrict the hedonistic nature of human action by way of numerous rules and regulations telling us what we can and cannot do although, in fact, these rules and regulations have no rational justification and not primarily the result of the basic principles of the protection of others and their property[13];
- the impact on a society of existing moral principles which arose in completely different times and which are completely inconsistent with the present day;
- the impact of the dominant religion, whose representatives often assume the right to determine certain rules of conduct for the whole

---

[13] I am referring to the fundamental principles of the law not to harm other people or their possessions, as advocated by John Locke.

society, regardless of the fact that only part of the society follows the said religion.

The following examples will illustrate the negative impact of the factors above. In the case of legal principles, there is the requirement to pay national social and health insurance on the basis of arbitrary rules imposed by the state. This obligation is a kind of state-sanctioned deprivation of liberty of its citizens and also a testament to its mismanagement of these funds, which leads to lower benefits and lack of adequate health care, as well as to the situation when citizens become both petitioners and beggars at the same time. Another example of this legal principle is the obligation to pay for a television license, which has no rational justification whatsoever. There is no reason for all citizens to contribute to a propaganda mouthpiece for politicians. If all these services were at the appropriate level, they should be part of a market game and be offered on the open market, just as similar services offered by private entities are. Another example is the ban on abortion, which sometimes leads to the fact that a woman who has been raped is forced to give birth to the child of the offender, someone who has done her terrible harm. Once again, the state knows best as to what the woman should do, allowing her no free choice and often sentencing her to mental suffering. In such a situation, the state becomes an ordinary criminal, violating the principle of the protection of another person. One may wonder who gave politicians the right to make decisions on the health and lives of women. Is there any reason to assume that women are people of a lower category, unable to think? That they are barbarians, wanting to get rid of unborn children for no valid reason? Nobody has the right to think so, and no one has the right to decide on the life and health of another person who is not mentally ill. Every person knows best what is good (desirable, beneficial) for them.

Further examples, this time related to the influence of culture, are the patriarchal model of the family, the belief that even minors should be put to hard work, no discussion of human sexuality, the denial of assertiveness or alienation of people with disabilities. Another example in this category is the social (cultural) view that the government is above the law, and that governance give the privilege of infallibility and that it means doing good[14]. The latter is especially dangerous because it leads to the enslavement of people and negates their pursuit of happiness.

An example of the influence of many religions is the negation of mortal life. The pursuit of personal happiness, possession of material goods or the pursuit of pleasure is denied. According to most religious doctrines, we should live a relatively ascetic life so that there might be the possibility of life after death. Another effect of this type is the negation of human sexual otherness, civil partnerships or unmarried people having children. These are obvious examples that contradict the nature of human action and the pursuit of happiness.

These examples do not mean that the socialization process has only a negative impact on the nature of human action; they show only exogenous factors limiting human hedonism. Many other factors, however, have a positive impact on life within social structures and on cooperation between people, cooperation which is of great importance for the quality of life and the achievement of goals which would be unattainable where one person acted alone. The most important conclusion from the above is that in the present-day world, human activity is limited by absurd principles of law or cultural influences, which clearly reduce the quality of life. It seems that it is high time we became aware of this and took action to change the situation.

---

[14] These principles of social behavior can be found in the results of studies on cultures carried out by the sociologist Geert Hofstede [2010].

6. THE HABIT LOOP – A BLESSING AND A CURSE

According to research, up to 40 % of everyday human activities are not the result of conscious decisions but of habits. What we order in restaurants, how we speak, whether we spend everything we earn or save for a rainy day, whether we do exercise, how we think and work – these are all habits of great importance for everyone's health, efficiency, financial security and happiness [Duhigg, 2012: 20]. It has been shown that, biologically, habits are formed in the deepest parts of the brain where the older, more primitive structures responsible for automatic behavior such as breathing, swallowing or fear are found. Habits are located towards the center of the brain, in oval cell structures called the basal ganglia [Duhigg, 2012: 42].

Habit can be represented in the form of a three-part loop (Fig. 6.1):

- ➢ A cue, or trigger, that orders the brain to switch to automatic mode and prompts it to run the relevant habit;
- ➢ A routine, which can be physical, mental or emotional;
- ➢ A reward, which is important for the recording component in the brain, that this habit is worth remembering.

After a habit has been formed, the brain ceases to make conscious decisions and everything starts to happen in the unconscious. Habit formation is an extremely important process for humans, without which we would not be able to think creatively, but would instead focus on basic life functions. On the other hand, habits are encoded in unconscious action maps (cognitive maps), which are based on the cue–reward (benefit, pleasure) diagram, which means that these actions are purely hedonistic.

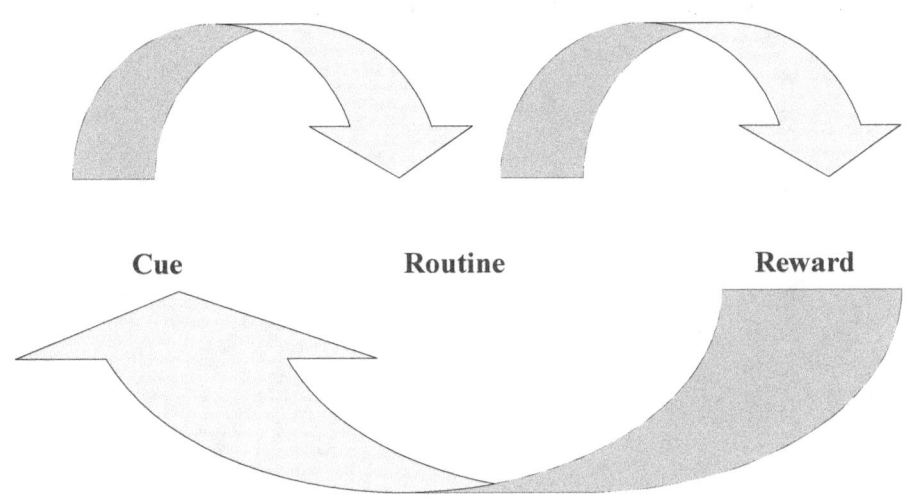

Fig. 6.1. The habit loop.
Source: Own work based on Duhigg, 2012: 49.

Based on research into the nature of habits, therefore, we can say that they control up to 40 % of behavior, are hedonistic in nature and are located in the unconscious. This is important information for the study of the nature of human action, since it means that many choices are habitual and so extremely difficult to change. If we follow the loop to create a habit, we can easily find that its origin is related to the nature of human action discussed above. The loop is formed where multiple rewards (benefits or pleasure, mitigating unpleasantness) occur after the specific activities, as a rule which is perpetuated in the mind (unconsciousness) in order to reward a specific action. Habits apply to all areas of human activity; as a result, it is extraordinarily difficult to change human tastes or judgments. On the one hand, habits make people's lives easier, and without them it would be extremely difficult for them to function, which indicates their positive impact on our lives, but on the other hand they are a curse when routines or judgments need to be changed.

7. LIMITATIONS TO THE HUMAN PURSUIT OF HAPPINESS

To sum up the current discussion on the nature of human action, we should consider what stands in the way of the human pursuit of happiness, and what action people need to take to achieve the highest possible quality of life. First of all, it must be assumed that human activity is always a subjective desire for happiness, and no one has the right to point out (or argue) what would make another person happier. In this sense, the criterion of less or more satisfaction does not exist beyond a particular individual's own subjective assessment. Everyone has their own motives and desires and from their own point of view their actions are always rational.

Using my axiom of human action and research on human nature, the following picture of humans emerges:

- everyone has a different, subjective perception of good and evil, benefit and pleasure, and loss and unpleasantness;
- humans have an aversion to the risk of loss;
- humans consciously choose between immediate and long-term benefits, i.e. they are inherently responsible and seek to secure their future;
- humans are susceptible to the effects of the socialization process, which has an impact on changes to their definition of benefit or pleasure and leads to action which is not always aimed at directly satisfying their own desires;

- unconscious processes, in particular those conditioned by habit loops, have an advantage over conscious decision-making processes;
- drives, instincts and emotions are critical and often "rule" humans at decision-making moments;
- humans are lazy, have an aversion to work and try to divide it;
- freedom of choice is a core value for most people.

Considering the research methodology, based on Imre Lakatos' methodological research system, we have a hard core theorem and auxiliary hypotheses in a protective belt. To determine what the major obstacles and constraints in the above-accepted model of human pursuit of happiness are, below is a diagram (sequence) of human action, with its form referring to the methodological assumptions:

> **Every person who is not in a vegetative state and is not mentally ill takes action, the motive for which is unpleasantness and its removal is the goal of the action. Every action also seeks happiness, because the elimination of all causes of unpleasantness result in a higher quality of life. People use reason in order to meet their needs and desires (mitigating unpleasantness) and do so consciously.**

THE NATURE OF HUMAN ACTION

UNPLEASANTNESS:

Physical – the failure to achieve lower-order needs
(or those resulting from a comparison of one's own state to the state of others)
Psychological – the failure to achieve higher-order needs
(or those resulting from a comparison of one's own state to the state of others)

THE A PRIORI AXIOM OF HUMAN ACTION BY L. VON MISES (HARD CORE THEOREM)

To achieve the aim which subjectively had the greatest value among all initial aims.

To act or refrain from acting, which means the use of scarce resources in the form of at least the body of one person and their time.

The resources used have a certain value for the person acting and that person must be careful that the use of these resources is necessary to achieve the desired aim.

These actions must be performed one after the other in time and represent the decision to act in a way that allows us to expect that we will achieve the most valued aim and to postpone the achievement of less desirable aims at the given time.

The result of prioritizing one aim over the others is that costs are incurred in that alternative aims cannot be achieved.

At the outset, the chosen aim must be assigned a higher value than its cost and the expected benefit (pleasure) from achieving it (evaluated as the value of the foregone possibility to achieve alternative aims).

The action is threatened with loss if the person acting discovers at a future time that the goal achieved has a lower value than that which would have been obtained through achieving the alternative, rejected, aims.

Limitations of the surroundings:

- the socialization process,

- the State; social, legal, political, economic systems

The influence of human nature:

- habits

- accepted axiom of the hedonistic nature of human action (auxiliary hypotheses)

Anything that restricts a person's free choice is contrary to their desire for happiness, the nature of their existence, and the nature of their every action

The hedonism of human action

Positive hedonism – the result of the action is of something desired, beneficial both for the person acting and their surroundings; or when the result is something desired, beneficial for the person acting and neutral to the environment.

Negative hedonism – the result of the action is something desired and beneficial for the person acting, but has undesirable and adverse effects on their surroundings.

THE ELIMINATION OF UNPLEASANTNESS – INCREASE IN THE QUALITY OF LIFE

The key issue in the diagram is to determine the most relevant, external limitations of human action. Just by knowing what stands in the way of the human pursuit of happiness makes it possible to find ways to change this state of affairs. As a general rule, all our needs and desires are transformed into unpleasantness, which is either physical or mental. Limitations encountered on the way to eliminating them arise primarily in our environment and are imposed by the state, and in particular by the legal, economic, political and social systems in force. In this sense, the state can nullify or support the human pursuit of happiness. For this reason, the state must be subjected to particular analysis. All other limitations result either from the process of socialization or from human nature, so we have little scope to eliminate their impact on human activity. Here the most important issue seems be every individual's adequate knowledge of these processes in order to be able to at least partially control this impact. By understanding the processes of socialization and the formation of the habit loop, a person can consciously mitigate the adverse consequences of their impact on their own performance. In contrast, where the state is involved, people need both knowledge of its adverse influence as well as an understanding of how it operates and need to know what can possibly be changed and how this should be done.

8. HEDONISM IN TREE DIMENSIONS

According to the findings, the hedonistic nature of human action generally favors the pursuit of happiness. Human hedonism also affects the functioning of the different social structures. The essence of human activity, in particular its hedonic nature, has consequences for human activities in the following dimensions (areas):

- ➢ individual – usually occurs as positive hedonism;
- ➢ organizational – appears in two forms, both as positive and negative hedonism;
- ➢ political – usually manifests itself as negative hedonism.

Individual hedonism has already been discussed in previous sections of this article. It should generally be presumed that it has a positive impact on the development of civilization and the standard of living of every human being and does not entail any significant adverse effects that are felt by other people. Due to the subjective nature of pleasure, there are people for whom the pursuit of pleasure may prove detrimental to their surroundings. Usually, however, the pursuit of pleasure by individuals has a positive impact on the lives of others. This hedonism requires us to work with others to achieve our needs, and this cooperation is usually beneficial to all parties and provides everyone with benefits or pleasure.

Organizational hedonism is the external activities of an organization which are achieved through the decisions of those with the appropriate legitimacy to take decisions. It should be emphasized that each organization, just as any society, is not a real living entity but simply a group of individuals belonging to a given organizational structure. It is not the organization which acts but the people who have the appropriate authority to take decisions within the organization, shaping its principles of operation. Just as each person acts according to the axiom here described, so does the organization by implementing the decisions taken by the decision-makers.

The external action of the organization, which is a reflection of the hedonistic nature of its decision-makers, is also hedonistic in nature. Hedonism leads to benefits, both for the decision-makers and for the organization itself, which is usually reflected in financial results enabling its long-term existence. This activity has both positive and negative effects on the organization's surroundings. On the one hand, the organization is a place of work and produces new goods and services for many consumers. Provided it is not a state monopoly[15] or does not participate in price fixing, it provides the market with desired products at the best possible price and strives for the optimal use of resources. On the other hand, there have been numerous cases highlighting the negative effects of organizational hedonism, such as abandoning the production of drugs for rare diseases as this is too costly, the corruption of doctors, funded by the pharmaceutical companies in order to increase drug sales, the sale of long-term investment plans to the elderly, who are unlikely to live to see them come to term, or environmental degradation resulting from externalizing common goods.

Political hedonism is a complex problem resulting from the actions of a small (but growing) number of people involved in politics and associated with the state administration at all levels of government. This concerns a specific time period of governance

---

[15] In the situation where the organization belongs to the state and legal regulations do not permit other entities to enter the market

(term of office), as well as a large, randomly-chosen group of people often lacking relevant qualifications, as well as the problem of the ownership of the assets they are managing. Public goods are regarded as belonging to no-one, and which are not as well taken care of as one's own goods[16]. These people, often unqualified, sometimes without any assets of their own, act only and in such a way as to meet their own needs, and not in order to achieve aims for the whole of society. These are the parasitic activities of people who use funds taken from the rest of society, i.e. taxes, and decide how this public money is to be spent without incurring any responsibility. They are not "super-humans" and the hedonistic axiom of human action affects them in particular. There is therefore nothing to prevent them channeling their efforts primarily for their own benefit or pleasure. Unfortunately, they do so at the expense of society as a whole, which is clearly negative and has harmful effects. A quick browse of the day's news sites will uncover new cases of corruption, fraud or the waste of more millions of dollars. Not uncommon are stories of the relationship of business with the world of politics and how public tenders are fixed and public contracts awarded to "friendly" companies. Since, in today's democracies, government officials (politicians) are responsible for spending 50 % of all revenue, the scale of these parasitic activities is huge. In addition, it is very rare for someone to suffer the consequences of their actions, even if there has been wastage on a large scale. This social group apparently takes the rest of society for fools that can be endlessly robbed and for whom they can decide what is good and what is bad. People in power consider themselves the better part of society, whom the rest must treat with the appropriate respect. They forget the fact that they live at the expense of others and do not produce any goods or added value to the economy.

---

[16] Public goods are understood as state property and own goods are understood as goods belonging to private owners

9. CONCLUSION

To conclude our reflections on the nature of human action, we must stress that it is deterministic. Wolf Singer, Gerhard Roth, Hans J. Markowitsch and Wolfgang Prinz long ago confirmed the thesis that free will is a fiction. The primary function of consciousness is not, as is usually assumed, the control of behavior, but rather providing the human "I" and its surrounding environment with convincing reasons as to why it behaved or behaves in one way rather than another [Schmidt-Salomon, 2013: 93]. Note, however, that free will, which does not exist, is not the same as the act of choice over our actions. Although the latter phenomenon is deterministic in nature, this determinism results from all the external and internal factors affecting the person making the decision, and these are largely dependent on earlier events in a person's life.

"Free will" as a scientific theoretical construct has not yet been a subject of interest to sociology or psychology. Despite all the differences between Sigmund Freud, the precursor of psychoanalysis, and Burrhus Frederic Skinner, the founder of behaviorism, both of them agreed that that something as odd as "free will" has no raison d'être [Schmidt-Salomon, 2013: 99].

Gerhard Roth was of a similar opinion:

> [...] The conscious, thinking and free-willed "I" does not assume moral responsibility for what the brain does, even if it is deceived by it in most unscrupulous way. [...] The sometimes annoying feeling of guilt we

have when we have done something wrong is the result of an erroneous assumption that we, aka our conscious "I", are the cause of this deed. [...] The actions of a man, alongside genetic predispositions, are largely the product of the cognitive process passed on by the limbic system. The limbic system is guided by the [...] criteria of good / pleasant and bad / painful, and it does not judge behavior based on the needs of the conscious "I" but checks if in the past the effects of the same or similar decisions were positive or negative, and whether in relation to this they should be taken again or abandoned [Roth, 2003: 180; author's translation].

It follows that a person who, under exactly the same conditions, i.e. with the same external stimuli and internal behavioral priorities, could select both behavior A and B, would be the greatest magician the world has ever seen. More than a hundred years ago, Eduard Kohlrausch put it thus:

[...] the place of a man who, in precisely-defined external conditions and with a given state of mind could act both well and completely differently [...] is not in jail or in a psychiatric hospital, but in a glass case [...] so that everyone could admire him as the greatest and most incomprehensible anomaly that human eyes have ever set eyes upon [Kohlrausch, 1905: 98; author's translation].

Free will is different from freedom of action above all in that only the latter can be experienced sensually. Moments in which we unexpectedly experience it are exceptionally happy ones for us. While restrictions on our freedom of action have very obvious effects, we have no sense allowing us to feel the limits of our fictional free will. No-one is likely to perceive that there has been a restriction of liberty where, under the influence of determinants that shaped them, they choose precisely one thing over another, or simply reject what they do not want [Schmidt-Salomon 2013: 100]. For this reason, if people are deprived of freedom of choice, they are deprived of the only freedom they can realistically have.

The concept of the nature of human action as discussed here is based on both Mises's a priori axiom (hard core theorem), and my own detailed axiom system (auxiliary hypotheses). The human pursuit of happiness and the possibility to achieve it depend on whether the social systems in which they live are conducive to their aspirations. To conclude, it is worth considering whether the hypotheses posed at the beginning of the article have been confirmed. These were:

T1: Human action is of a hedonistic nature, which implies numerous theories in economics and management science and in particular allows many theories of consumer behavior to be confirmed.

T2: The hedonistic nature of human action is reflected in three spheres, personal, political and organizational, with political hedonism an inherent feature of the political classes, entailing negative consequences for the whole of society, in particular leading to the misallocation of all resources and the inability to achieve optimal quality of life.

Has the discussion in this chapter confirmed the hypotheses? I believe so, but in the social sciences there is always the problem of unequivocal proof. Prediction in most social science theories is very limited, because we are never dealing with the same external conditions, making it impossible to conduct research experiments. An important argument in favor of the confirmation of these hypotheses is their compatibility with many economic theories and hypotheses, including in the field of consumer behavior, which are currently accepted by most economists. These theories were the starting point for the axiom system. Another factor confirming the hypotheses were the results of the research experiment and selected research in evolutionary biology and neuroscience.

The adoption of the hypotheses I propose here should result in a new approach to the study of human action, and in particular of consumer behavior, and new insights into issues on the quality of life.

BIBLIOGRAPHY

Bauman Z. (2009), *Sztuka życia*, tr.. T. Kunz, Wydawnictwo Literackie, Kraków.

Chodorov F. (1959), *The Rise and Fall of Society,* Devin Adair, New York.

Duhigg, Ch. (2012), *The Power of Habit: Why We Do What We Do in Life and Business*, Random House, New York.

Green A.W. (1968), *The Reified Villain*, Social Research, vol. 35, No. 4, pp. 651 – 665.

Hayek F.A. (2005), *The Road to Serfdom*, The Institute of Economic Affairs, London.

Hofstede G., Hofstede G.J., Minkov M. (2010), *Cultures and Organizations: Software of the Mind: Intercultural Cooperation and Its Importance for Survival*, McGraw-Hill, New York.

Hoppe G. (2014), *The Model of Hedonistic Human Being versus the Social Responsibility of Consumers*, CreateSpace Independent Publishing Platform, New York.

Hoppe H.H. (2006), *The Economics and Ethics of Private Property. Studies in Political Economy and Philosophy*, online edition by The Ludwig von Mises Institute.

Kast B. (2007), *Wie der Bauch dem Kopf beim Denken hilft. Die Kraft der Intuition*, Frankfurt am Main.

Kohlrausch E. (1905), *Der Kampf der Kriminalistenschulen im Lichte des Falles Dippold*, Monatsschrift für Kriminalpsychologie und Strafrechtsreform, 1.

Kozielecki, J. (2000), *Koncepcje psychologiczne człowieka*, Wydawnictwo Akademickie Żak, Warsaw.

Lakatos I. (1995), *Pisma z filozofii nauk empirycznych*, tr. W. Sady, W. Krajewski, PWN, Warsaw.

Marcuse L. (1973), *Argumente und Rezepte. Ein Wörterbuch für Zeitgenossen*, Zürich.

Maslow A. (1970), *Motivation and Personality*, Harper & Row, New York.

Mises L. von (1998), *Human Action. A Treatise on Economics [The Scholar's Edition]*, online edition by the Ludwig von Mises Institute.

Nietzsche F. (2002), *Beyond Good and Evil*, tr. Judith Norman, CUP, Cambridge.

Roth G. (2003), *Aus Sicht des Gehirns*, Suhrkamp, Frankfurt am Main.

Rothbard M.N. (2004), *For a New Liberty: The Libertarian Manifesto,* online edition by The Ludwig von Mises Institute.

Scheler M. (1998), *Ressentiment, tr. Louis A. Coser,* Marquette University Press, Milwaukee.

Schmidt-Salomon M. (2013), *Poza dobrem i złem*, tr. A. Lipiński, Dobra Literatura, Słupsk.

Tocqueville A. de (2006), *Democracy in America*, Volume 2, tr. H. Reeve, Project Gutenberg (Kindle Edition).

Zimbardo P., Boyd J. (2009), *The Time Paradox*, Free Press, New York.

www.ingramcontent.com/pod-product-compliance
Lightning Source LLC
Chambersburg PA
CBHW070329190526
45169CB00005B/1810